FIRST SPORT

GYMNASTICS

James Nixon

Photography by Bobby Humphrey

W

FRANKLIN WATTS
LONDON • SYDNEY

First published in 2014
by Franklin Watts

Copyright © Franklin Watts 2014

Franklin Watts
338 Euston Road
London NW1 3BH

Franklin Watts Australia
Level 17/207 Kent Street
Sydney, NSW 2000

Series Editor: Julia Bird
Planning and production by Discovery Books Ltd
Editor: James Nixon
Series designer: Ian Winton
Commissioned photography: Bobby Humphrey
Picture credits: Shutterstock: pp. 4 (Lilyana Vynogradova),
11 bottom (Lilyana Vynogradova), 13 top (Lilyana Vynogradova),
19 (Lilyana Vynogradova), 23 middle (Henry Stockton).

The author, packager and publisher would like to thank City of Birmingham
Gymnastics Club for their help and participation in this book.

Every attempt has been made to clear copyright.
Should there be any inadvertent omission please apply
to the publisher for rectification.

Dewey number 796.4'4
ISBN: 978 1 4451 2633 3
Library ebook ISBN: 978 1 4451 2637 1

Printed in China

Franklin Watts is a division of Hachette Children's Books,
an Hachette UK company.
www.hachette.co.uk

Contents

What is gymnastics?

Gymnastics is an exciting and spectacular sport. Gymnasts perform different movements and make shapes with their bodies.

They link moves together in amazing displays.

Gymnastics is done on pieces of equipment called **apparatus.** Boys and girls use a different set of apparatus.

In competitions, **judges** score the gymnasts for their displays.

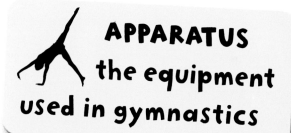

APPARATUS
the equipment used in gymnastics

JUDGE
a person who decides the results of a competition

5

Starting out

A gymnast's clothes have to be close-fitting so that the gymnast can move freely. Girls wear a leotard. Boys wear shorts, or trousers called 'longs', over the top of a leotard.

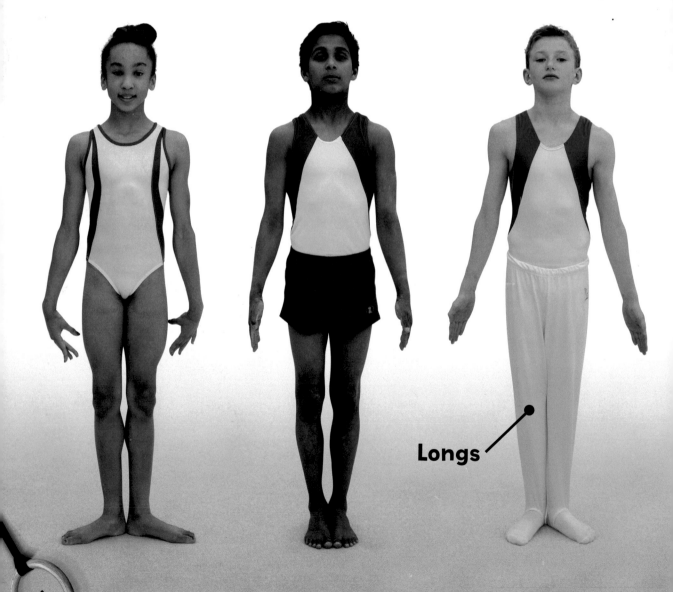

Longs

Gymnasts need to be strong and **flexible.** They do exercises and stretches to train their bodies.

FLEXIBLE
able to bend
the body easily

Making arch shapes like this with your body will make you a stronger gymnast.

Basic skills

Rolls are important skills to learn in gymnastics. You can do them forwards and backwards.

Backward and forward rolls should be smooth, with the body tucked into a neat and tight shape.

Learning to do the **splits** will make you more flexible.

SPLITS
when you stretch your legs out either side of you

Beginners can start with a half splits like this. Each time you practise it, you will find it easier.

Handstands and cartwheels

The handstand is the most important gymnastic skill of all. Handstand shapes can be made on all of the apparatus.

To do a good handstand you must hold your body straight and still.

Once you can do a handstand, you are ready to learn how to cartwheel. This is when you swing your legs over your head to travel sideways.

Top gymnasts can cartwheel without putting their hands down at all!

On the floor

On the floor, gymnasts put together a series of spins, leaps, beautiful shapes and acrobatic **tumbles**. These **routines** are exciting to watch.

TUMBLES
a series of flips across the floor using only the hands and feet

The floor mat is springy to help gymnasts jump high into the air.

Girls set their floor routines to music and add dance moves.

ROUTINE
a series of moves that make up a gymnastic performance

Vaulting

A vault is a short but spectacular performance. The gymnast sprints down a runway, bounces off a springboard and **somersaults** powerfully over the vaulting table.

Runway

Springboard

Vaulting table

SOMERSAULT
spin head over heels in mid-air

To do the most difficult vaults, gymnasts add twists and turns as they fly through the air.

The hardest part is to land safely with two feet on the ground!

The beam and pommel horse

Girls do gymnastic routines on a long, thin **beam.** On the beam, you need to be confident, brave and, above all, have good balance.

Gymnasts can perform acrobatic leaps and spins on the beam without wobbling.

BEAM
a padded plank of wood set over one metre high in the air

One of the hardest apparatus for boys is the **pommel horse.** Great strength is needed to hold your body in place as you swing your legs around, lifting each hand as you turn.

POMMEL HORSE a padded table with handles fitted on the top

The high bars

On the high bar, boys perform amazing routines. They swing and twist on the bar in giant circles.

High bar

The most spectacular moves are when the gymnast lets go of the bar and catches it again.

Girls use an apparatus called the **asymmetric bars** and jump from one bar to the other. To get top marks from the judges, the swings and jumps should flow without any stopping.

ASYMMETRIC BARS
two bars some distance apart, with one bar higher than the other

Parallel bars and rings

On the **parallel bars** and rings, boys use their strength to hold their bodies still in position.

Gymnasts swing themselves into positions above and below the parallel bars.

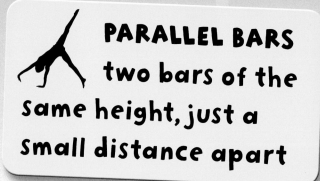

PARALLEL BARS two bars of the same height, just a small distance apart

On the rings, the gymnast has to hold shapes for a number of seconds. This boy is performing an 'L' shape.

All routines need to finish with a tidy landing. To land, the gymnast lets go of the rings and somersaults through the air.

Rings

Rhythmic gymnastics

Rhythmic gymnastics is a different type of gymnastics. The gymnasts dance and move to music on the floor, while using equipment such as balls, hoops, clubs and ribbons.

The ribbon can be **twirled** to make beautiful shapes.

TWIRLED
spun around quickly in a circle

The hoop can be rolled and moved over and around the gymnast's body.

The ball is balanced on parts of the body with great skill.

Club

Gymnasts can throw clubs, balls and hoops high into the air. They catch them at the same time as doing leaps and somersaults!

Index